East and West

Bret Harte

Contents

Part I. East and West Poems. 7
A Greyport Legend. 7
A Newport Romance. 9
The Hawk's Nest. 12
In the Mission Garden. Father Felipe. 14
Pachita (briskly). The Old Major Explains. 16
"Seventy-Nine" Mr. Interviewer Interviewed. 17
His Answer to "Her Letter." Reported by Truthful James. 19
Further Language from Truthful James. (Nye's Ford, Stanislaus.) 22
The Wonderful Spring of San Joaquin. 25
On a Cone of the Big Trees. Sequoia Gigantea. 29
A Sanitary Message. 31
The Copperhead. 33
On a Pen of Thomas Starr King. 34
Lone Mountain. (Cemetery, San Francisco.) 35
California's Greeting to Seward. 36
The Two Ships. 37
The Goddess. For the Sanitary Fair. 38
Address. 40
The Lost Galleon. 42
A Second Review of the Grand Army. 48

Part II Before the Curtain. 51
The Stage-Driver's Story. 52
Aspiring Miss de Laine. A Chemical Narrative. 54
California Madrigal. On the Approach of Spring. 60
St. Thomas. A Geographical Survey. 61
The Ballad of Mr. Cooke. A Legend of the Cliff House, San Francisco. 64
The Legends of the Rhine. 69
Mrs. Judge Jenkins. 71
Avitor. An Aerial Retrospect. 73
A White-Pine Ballad. 75
Moral. What the Wolf Really Said to Little Red Riding-Hood. 76
The Ritualist. By a Communicant of "St. James's." 77
A Moral Vindicator. 78
Songs Without Sense. 80
For the Parlor and Piano. 80
I.--The Personified Sentimental. 80
II.--The Homely Pathetic. 81
III.--Swiss Air. 82

EAST AND WEST

BY

Bret Harte

Part I.
East and West Poems.

A Greyport Legend.

(1797.)

They ran through the streets of the seaport town;
They peered from the decks of the ships that lay:
The cold sea-fog that came whitening down
Was never as cold or white as they.
 "Ho, Starbuck and Pinckney and Tenterden!
  Run for your shallops, gather your men,
  Scatter your boats on the lower bay."

Good cause for fear! In the thick midday
The hulk that lay by the rotting pier,
Filled with the children in happy play,
Parted its moorings, and drifted clear,--
  Drifted clear beyond the reach or call,--
  Thirteen children they were in all,--
    All adrift in the lower bay!

Said a hard-faced skipper, "God help us all!
She will not float till the turning tide!"
Said his wife, "My darling will hear *my* call,
Whether in sea or heaven she bide:"
  And she lifted a quavering voice and high,
  Wild and strange as a sea-bird's cry,
    Till they shuddered and wondered at her side.

The fog drove down on each laboring crew,
Veiled each from each and the sky and shore:
There was not a sound but the breath they drew,
And the lap of water and creak of oar;
  And they felt the breath of the downs, fresh blown
  O'er leagues of clover and cold gray stone,
    But not from the lips that had gone before.

They come no more. But they tell the tale,
That, when fogs are thick on the harbor reef,
The mackerel fishers shorten sail;
For the signal they know will bring relief:
  For the voices of children, still at play
  In a phantom hulk that drifts alway
    Through channels whose waters never fail.

It is but a foolish shipman's tale,
A theme for a poet's idle page;
But still, when the mists of doubt prevail,
And we lie becalmed by the shores of Age,
  We hear from the misty troubled shore
  The voice of the children gone before,
    Drawing the soul to its anchorage.

A Newport Romance.

They say that she died of a broken heart
  (I tell the tale as 'twas told to me);
But her spirit lives, and her soul is part
  Of this sad old house by the sea.

Her lover was fickle and fine and French:
  It was nearly a hundred years ago
When he sailed away from her arms--poor wench--
  With the Admiral Rochambeau.

I marvel much what periwigged phrase
  Won the heart of this sentimental Quaker,
At what golden-laced speech of those modish days
  She listened--the mischief take her!

But she kept the posies of mignonette
  That he gave; and ever as their bloom failed
And faded (though with her tears still wet)
  Her youth with their own exhaled.

Till one night, when the sea-fog wrapped a shroud
  Round spar and spire and tarn and tree,
Her soul went up on that lifted cloud
  From this sad old house by the sea.

And ever since then, when the clock strikes two,
  She walks unbidden from room to room,
And the air is filled that she passes through
  With a subtle, sad perfume.

The delicate odor of mignonette,
  The ghost of a dead and gone bouquet,
Is all that tells of her story; yet
  Could she think of a sweeter way?

*   *   *   *   *

I sit in the sad old house to-night,--
  Myself a ghost from a farther sea;
And I trust that this Quaker woman might,
  In courtesy, visit me.

For the laugh is fled from porch and lawn,
  And the bugle died from the fort on the hill,
And the twitter of girls on the stairs is gone,
  And the grand piano is still.

Somewhere in the darkness a clock strikes two;
  And there is no sound in the sad old house,
But the long veranda dripping with dew,
  And in the wainscot a mouse.

The light of my study-lamp streams out
  From the library door, but has gone astray
In the depths of the darkened hall. Small doubt
  But the Quakeress knows the way.

Was it the trick of a sense o'erwrought
  With outward watching and inward fret?
But I swear that the air just now was fraught
  With the odor of mignonette!

I open the window, and seem almost--

So still lies the ocean--to hear the beat
Of its Great Gulf artery off the coast,
  And to bask in its tropic heat.

In my neighbor's windows the gas-lights flare,
  As the dancers swing in a waltz of Strauss;
And I wonder now could I fit that air
  To the song of this sad old house.

And no odor of mignonette there is
  But the breath of morn on the dewy lawn;
And mayhap from causes as slight as this
  The quaint old legend is born.

But the soul of that subtle, sad perfume,
  As the spiced embalmings, they say, outlast
The mummy laid in his rocky tomb,
  Awakens my buried past.

And I think of the passion that shook my youth,
  Of its aimless loves and its idle pains,
And am thankful now for the certain truth
  That only the sweet remains.

And I hear no rustle of stiff brocade,
  And I see no face at my library door;
For now that the ghosts of my heart are laid,
  She is viewless forevermore.

But whether she came as a faint perfume,
  Or whether a spirit in stole of white,
I feel, as I pass from the darkened room,
  She has been with my soul to-night!

The Hawk's Nest.

(Sierras.)

We checked our pace,--the red road sharply rounding;
  We heard the troubled flow
Of the dark olive depths of pines, resounding
  A thousand feet below.

Above the tumult of the canon lifted,
  The gray hawk breathless hung;
Or on the hill a winged shadow drifted
  Where furze and thorn-bush clung;

Or where half-way the mountain side was furrowed
  With many a seam and scar;
Or some abandoned tunnel dimly burrowed,--
  A mole-hill seen so far.

We looked in silence down across the distant
  Unfathomable reach:
A silence broken by the guide's consistent
  And realistic speech.

"Walker of Murphy's blew a hole through Peters
  For telling him he lied;
Then up and dusted out of South Hornitos
  Across the long Divide.

"We ran him out of Strong's, and up through Eden,
  And 'cross the ford below;

And up this canon (Peters' brother leadin'),
  And me and Clark and Joe.

"He fou't us game: somehow, I disremember
  Jest how the thing kem round;
Some say 'twas wadding, some a scattered ember
  From fires on the ground.

"But in one minute all the hill below him
  Was just one sheet of flame;
Guardin' the crest, Sam Clark and I called to him.
  And,--well, the dog was game!

"He made no sign: the fires of hell were round him,
  The pit of hell below.
We sat and waited, but never found him;
  And then we turned to go.

"And then--you see that rock that's grown so bristly
  With chaparral and tan--
Suthin' crep' out: it might hev been a grizzly,
  It might hev been a man;

"Suthin' that howled, and gnashed its teeth, and shouted
  In smoke and dust and flame;
Suthin' that sprang into the depths about it,
  Grizzly or man,--but game!

"That's all. Well, yes, it does look rather risky,
  And kinder makes one queer
And dizzy looking down. A drop of whiskey
  Ain't a bad thing right here!"

In the Mission Garden.

(1865.)

Father Felipe.

I speak not the English well, but Pachita
She speak for me; is it not so, my Pancha?
Eh, little rogue? Come, salute me the stranger
        Americano.

Sir, in my country we say, "Where the heart is,
There live the speech." Ah! you not understand? So!
Pardon an old man,--what you call "ol fogy,"--
        Padre Felipe!

Old, Senor, old! just so old as the Mission.
You see that pear-tree? How old you think, Senor?
Fifteen year? Twenty? Ah, Senor, just ***Fifty***
        Gone since I plant him!

You like the wine? It is some at the Mission,
Made from the grape of the year Eighteen Hundred;
All the same time when the earthquake he come to
        San Juan Bautista.

But Pancha is twelve, and she is the rose-tree;
And I am the olive, and this is the garden:

And Pancha we say; but her name is Francisca,
        Same like her mother.

Eh, you knew ***her***? No? Ah! it is a story;
But I speak not, like Pachita, the English:
So? If I try, you will sit here beside me,
        And shall not laugh, eh?

When the American come to the Mission,
Many arrive at the house of Francisca:
One,--he was fine man,--he buy the cattle
        Of Jose Castro.

So! he came much, and Francisca she saw him:
And it was Love,--and a very dry season;
And the pears bake on the tree,--and the rain come,
        But not Francisca;

Not for one year; and one night I have walk much
Under the olive-tree, when comes Francisca:
Comes to me here, with her child, this Francisca,--
        Under the olive-tree.

Sir, it was sad; ... but I speak not the English;
So! ... she stay here, and she wait for her husband
He come no more, and she sleep on the hillside;
        There stands Pachita.

Ah! there's the Angelus. Will you not enter?
Or shall you walk in the garden with Pancha?
Go, little rogue--stt--attend to the stranger.
        Adios, Senor.

Pachita (briskly).

So, he's been telling that yarn about mother!
Bless you, he tells it to every stranger:
Folks about yer say the old man's my father;
      What's your opinion?

The Old Major Explains.

(Re-Union Army of the Potomac, 12th May, 1871.)

"Well, you see, the fact is, Colonel, I don't know as I can come:
For the farm is not half planted, and there's work to do at home;
And my leg is getting troublesome,--it laid me up last fall,
And the doctors, they have cut and hacked, and never found the ball.

"And then, for an old man like me, it's not exactly right,
This kind o' playing soldier with no enemy in sight.
'The Union,'--that was well enough way up to '66;
But this 'Re-Union,'--maybe now it's mixed with politics?

"No? Well, you understand it best; but then, you see, my lad,
I'm deacon now, and some might think that the example's bad.
And week from next is Conference…. You said the 12th of May?
Why, that's the day we broke their line at Spottsylvan-i-a!

"Hot work; eh, Colonel, wasn't it? Ye mind that narrow front:
They called it the 'Death-Angle!' Well, well, my lad, we won't
Fight that old battle over now: I only meant to say
I really can't engage to come upon the 12th of May.

"How's Thompson? What! will he be there? Well, now, I want to know!
The first man in the rebel works! they called him 'Swearing Joe:'
A wild young fellow, sir, I fear the rascal was; but then--
Well, short of heaven, there wa'n't a place he dursn't lead his men.

"And Dick, you say, is coming too. And Billy? ah! it's true
We buried him at Gettysburg: I mind the spot; do you?
A little field below the hill,--it must be green this May;
Perhaps that's why the fields about bring him to me to-day.

"Well, well, excuse me, Colonel! but there are some things that drop
The tail-board out one's feelings; and the only way's to stop.
So they want to see the old man; ah, the rascals! do they, eh?
Well, I've business down in Boston about the 12th of May."

"Seventy-Nine"
Mr. Interviewer Interviewed.

Know me next time when you see me, won't you, old smarty?
Oh, I mean you, old figger-head,--just the same party!
Take out your pensivil, d--n you; sharpen it, do!
Any complaints to make? Lots of 'em--one of 'em's *you*.

You! who are you, anyhow, goin' round in that sneakin' way?
Never in jail before, was you, old blatherskite, say?
Look at it; don't it look pooty? Oh, grin, and be d--d to you, do!
But, if I had you this side o' that gratin', I'd just make it lively
   for you.

How did I get in here? Well, what 'ud you give to know?
'Twasn't by sneakin' round where I hadn't no call to go.
'Twasn't by hangin' round a spyin' unfortnet men.
Grin! but I'll stop your jaw if ever you do that agen.

Why don't you say suthin', blast you? Speak your mind if you dare.
Ain't I a bad lot, sonny? Say it, and call it square.
Hain't got no tongue, hey, hev ye. O guard! here's a little swell,
A cussin' and swearin' and yellin', and bribin' me not to tell.

There, I thought that 'ud fetch ye. And you want to know my name?
"Seventy-Nine" they call me; but that is their little game.
For I'm werry highly connected, as a gent, sir, can understand;
And my family hold their heads up with the very furst in the land.

For 'twas all, sir, a put-up job on a pore young man like me;
And the jury was bribed a puppos, and aftdrst they couldn't agree.
And I sed to the judge, sez I,--Oh, grin! it's all right my son!
But you're a werry lively young pup, and you ain't to be played upon!

Wot's that you got--tobacco? I'm cussed but I thought 'twas a tract.
Thank ye. A chap t'other day--now, look'ee, this is a fact,
Slings me a tract on the evils o' keepin' bad company,
As if all the saints was howlin' to stay here along's we.

No: I hain't no complaints. Stop, yes; do you see that chap,--
Him standin' over there,--a hidin' his eves in his cap?

Well, that man's stumick is weak, and he can't stand the pris'n fare;
For the coffee is just half beans, and the sugar ain't no where.

Perhaps it's his bringin' up; but he sickens day by day,
And he doesn't take no food, and I'm seein' him waste away.
And it isn't the thing to see; for, whatever he's been and done,
Starvation isn't the plan as he's to be saved upon.

For he cannot rough it like me; and he hasn't the stamps, I guess,
To buy him his extry grub outside o' the pris'n mess.
And perhaps if a gent like you, with whom I've been sorter free,
Would--thank you! But, say, look here! Oh, blast it, don't give it to ME!

Don't you give it to me; now, don't ye, don't ye, don't!
You think it's a put-up job; so I'll thank ye, sir, if you won't.
But hand him the stamps yourself: why, he isn't even my pal;
And if it's a comfort to you, why, I don't intend that he shall.

His Answer to "Her Letter." Reported by Truthful James.

Being asked by an intimate party,--
  Which the same I would term as a friend,--
Which his health it were vain to call hearty,
  Since the mind to deceit it might lend;
For his arm it was broken quite recent,
  And has something gone wrong with his lung,--
Which is why it is proper and decent

I should write what he runs off his tongue:

First, he says, Miss, he's read through your letter
  To the end,--and the end came too soon;
That a slight illness kept him your debtor
  (Which for weeks he was wild as a loon);
That his spirits are buoyant as yours is;
  That with you, Miss, he challenges Fate
(Which the language that invalid uses
  At times it were vain to relate).

And he says that the mountains are fairer
  For once being held in your thought;
That each rock holds a wealth that is rarer
  Than ever by gold-seeker sought
(Which are words he would put in these pages,
  By a party not given to guile;
Which the same not, at date, paying wages,
  Might produce in the sinful a smile).

He remembers the ball at the Ferry,
  And the ride, and the gate, and the vow,
And the rose that you gave him,--that very
  Same rose he is treasuring now
(Which his blanket he's kicked on his trunk, Miss,
  And insists on his legs being free;
And his language to me from his bunk, Miss,
  Is frequent and painful and free);

He hopes you are wearing no willows,
  But are happy and gay all the while;
That he knows (which this dodging of pillows
  Imparts but small ease to the style,

And the same you will pardon),--he knows, Miss,
    That, though parted by many a mile,
  Yet were he lying under the snows, Miss,
    They'd melt into tears at your smile.

  And you'll still think of him in your pleasures,
    In your brief twilight dreams of the past;
  In this green laurel-spray that he treasures,
    It was plucked where your parting was last;
  In this specimen,--but a small trifle,--
    It will do for a pin for your shawl
  (Which the truth not to wickedly stifle
    Was his last week's "clean up,"--and ***his all***).

  He's asleep, which the same might seem strange, Miss,
    Were it not that I scorn to deny
  That I raised his last dose, for a change, Miss,
    In view that his fever was high;
  But he lies there quite peaceful and pensive.
    And now, my respects, Miss, to you;
  Which my language, although comprehensive,
    Might seem to be freedom,--it's true.

  Which I have a small favor to ask you,
    As concerns a bull-pup, which the same,--
  If the duty would not overtask you,--
    You would please to procure for me, ***game***;
  And send per express to the Flat, Miss,
    Which they say York is famed for the breed,
  Which though words of deceit may be that, Miss,
    I'll trust to your taste, Miss, indeed.

P.S.--Which this same interfering
  Into other folks' way I despise;
Yet if it so be I was hearing
  That it's just empty pockets as lies
Betwixt you and Joseph, it follers,
  That, having no family claims,
Here's my pile; which it's six hundred dollars,
  As is yours, with respects,

        Truthful James.

Further Language from Truthful James.
(Nye's Ford, Stanislaus.)

(1870.)

Do I sleep? do I dream?
Do I wonder and doubt?
Are things what they seem?
Or is visions about?
Is our civilization a failure?
Or is the Caucasian played out?

Which expressions are strong;
Yet would feebly imply
Some account of a wrong--
Not to call it a lie--
As was worked off on William, my pardner,

And the same being W. Nye.

He came down to the Ford
On the very same day
Of that lottery drawed
By those sharps at the Bay;
And he says to me, "Truthful, how goes it?"
I replied, "It is far, far from gay;

"For the camp has gone wild
On this lottery game,
And has even beguiled
'Injin Dick' by the same."
Which said Nye to me, "Injins is pizen:
Do you know what his number is, James?"

I replied "7,2,
9,8,4, is his hand;"
When he started, and drew
Out a list, which he scanned;
Then he softly went for his revolver
With language I cannot command.

Then I said, "William Nye!"
But he turned upon me,
And the look in his eye
Was quite painful to see;
And he says, "You mistake: this poor Injin
I protects from such sharps as you be!"

I was shocked and withdrew;
But I grieve to relate,
When he next met my view

Injin Dick was his mate,
And the two around town was a-lying
In a frightfully dissolute state.

Which the war-dance they had
Round a tree at the Bend
Was a sight that was sad;
And it seemed that the end
Would not justify the proceedings,
As I quiet remarked to a friend.

For that Injin he fled
The next day to his band;
And we found William spread
Very loose on the strand,
With a peaceful-like smile on his features,
And a dollar greenback in his hand;

Which, the same when rolled out,
We observed with surprise,
That that Injin, no doubt,
Had believed was the prize,--
Them figures in red in the corner,
Which the number of notes specifies.

Was it guile, or a dream?
Is it Nye that I doubt?
Are things what they seem?
Or is visions about?
Is our civilization a failure?
Or is the Caucasian played out?

The Wonderful Spring of San Joaquin.

Of all the fountains that poets sing,--
Crystal, thermal, or mineral spring;
Ponce de Leon's Fount of Youth;
Wells with bottoms of doubtful truth;
In short, of all the springs of Time
That ever were flowing in fact or rhyme,
That ever were tasted, felt, or seen,--
There were none like the Spring of San Joaquin.

Anno Domini Eighteen-Seven,
Father Dominguez (now in heaven,--
Obiit, Eighteen twenty-seven)
Found the spring, and found it, too,
By his mule's miraculous cast of a shoe;
For his beast--a descendant of Balaam's ass--
Stopped on the instant, and would not pass.

The Padre thought the omen good,
And bent his lips to the trickling flood;
Then--as the chronicles declare,
On the honest faith of a true believer--
His cheeks, though wasted, lank, and bare,
Filled like a withered russet-pear
In the vacuum of a glass receiver,
And the snows that seventy winters bring
Melted away in that magic spring.

Such, at least, was the wondrous news
The Padre brought into Santa Cruz.

The Church, of course, had its own views
Of who were worthiest to use
The magic spring; but the prior claim
Fell to the aged, sick, and lame.
Far and wide the people came:
Some from the healthful Aptos creek
Hastened to bring their helpless sick;
Even the fishers of rude Soquel
Suddenly found they were far from well;
The brawny dwellers of San Lorenzo
Said, in fact, they had never been so:
And all were-ailing,--strange to say,--
From Pescadero to Monterey.

Over the mountain they poured in
With leathern bottles, and bags of skin;
Through the canons a motley throng
Trotted, hobbled, and limped along.
The fathers gazed at the moving scene
With pious joy and with souls serene;
And then--a result perhaps foreseen--
They laid out the Mission of San Joaquin.

Not in the eyes of Faith alone
The good effects of the waters shone;
But skins grew rosy, eyes waxed clear,
Of rough vacquero and muleteer;
Angular forms were rounded out,
Limbs grew supple, and waists grew stout;
And as for the girls,--for miles about
They had no equal! To this day,
From Pescadero to Monterey,
You'll still find eyes in which are seen

The liquid graces of San Joaquin.

There is a limit to human bliss,
And the Mission of San Joaquin had this;
None went abroad to roam or stay,
But they fell sick in the queerest way,--
A singular ***maladie du pays***,
With gastric symptoms: so they spent
Their days in a sensuous content;
Caring little for things unseen
Beyond their bowers of living green,--
Beyond the mountains that lay between
The world and the Mission of San Joaquin.

Winter passed, and the summer came:
The trunks of ***madrono*** all aflame,
Here and there through the underwood
Like pillars of fire starkly stood.
All of the breezy solitude
  Was filled with the spicing of pine and bay
And resinous odors mixed and blended,
  And dim and ghost-like far away
The smoke of the burning woods ascended.
Then of a sudden the mountains swam,
The rivers piled their floods in a dam.

The ridge above Los Gatos creek
  Arched its spine in a feline fashion;
The forests waltzed till they grew sick,
  And Nature shook in a speechless passion;
And, swallowed up in the earthquake's spleen,
The wonderful Spring of San Joaquin
Vanished, and never more was seen!

Two days passed: the Mission folk
Out of their rosy dream awoke.
Some of them looked a trifle white;
But that, no doubt, was from earthquake fright.
Three days: there was sore distress,
Headache, nausea, giddiness.
Four days: faintings, tenderness
Of the mouth and fauces; and in less
Than one week,--here the story closes;
We won't continue the prognosis,--
Enough that now no trace is seen
Of Spring or Mission of San Joaquin.

Moral.

You see the point? Don't be too quick
To break bad habits: better stick,
Like the Mission folk, to your *arsenic*.

On a Cone of the Big Trees.
Sequoia Gigantea.

Brown foundling of the Western wood,
  Babe of primeval wildernesses!
Long on my table thou hast stood
  Encounters strange and rude caresses;
Perchance contented with thy lot,
  Surroundings new and curious faces,
As though ten centuries were not
  Imprisoned in thy shining cases!

Thou bring'st me back the halcyon days
  Of grateful rest; the week of leisure,
The journey lapped in autumn haze,
  The sweet fatigue that seemed a pleasure,
The morning ride, the noonday halt,
  The blazing slopes, the red dust rising,
And then--the dim, brown, columned vault,
  With its cool, damp, sepulchral spicing.

Once more I see the rocking masts
  That scrape the sky, their only tenant
The jay-bird that in frolic casts
  From some high yard his broad blue pennant.
I see the Indian files that keep
  Their places in the dusty heather,
Their red trunks standing ankle deep
  In moccasins of rusty leather.

I see all this, and marvel much
  That thou, sweet woodland waif, art able
To keep the company of such
  As throng thy friend's--the poet's--table:
The latest spawn the press hath cast,--
  The "modern Pope's," "the later Byron's,"--
Why e'en the best may not outlast
  Thy poor relation,--Sempervirens.

Thy sire saw the light that shone
  On Mohammed's uplifted crescent,
On many a royal gilded throne
  And deed forgotten in the present;
He saw the age of sacred trees
  And Druid groves and mystic larches;
And saw from forest domes like these
  The builder bring his Gothic arches.

And must thou, foundling, still forego
  Thy heritage and high ambition,
To lie full lowly and full low,
  Adjusted to thy new condition?
Not hidden in the drifted snows,
  But under ink-drops idly spattered,
And leaves ephemeral as those
  That on thy woodland tomb were scattered.

Yet lie thou there, O friend! and speak
  The moral of thy simple story:
Though life is all that thou dost seek,
  And age alone thy crown of glory,--
Not thine the only germs that fail
  The purpose of their high creation,

If their poor tenements avail
  For worldly show and ostentation.

A Sanitary Message.

Last night, above the whistling wind,
  I heard the welcome rain,--
A fusillade upon the roof,
  A tattoo on the pane:
The key-hole piped; the chimney-top
  A warlike trumpet blew;
Yet, mingling with these sounds of strife,
  A softer voice stole through.

"Give thanks, O brothers!" said the voice,
  "That He who sent the rains
Hath spared your fields the scarlet dew
  That drips from patriot veins:
I've seen the grass on Eastern graves
  In brighter verdure rise;
But, oh! the rain that gave it life
  Sprang first from human eyes.

"I come to wash away no stain
  Upon your wasted lea;
I raise no banners, save the ones
  The forest wave to me:
Upon the mountain side, where Spring
  Her farthest picket sets,
My reveille awakes a host

Of grassy bayonets.

"I visit every humble roof;
  I mingle with the low:
Only upon the highest peaks
  My blessings fall in snow;
Until, in tricklings of the stream
  And drainings of the lea,
My unspent bounty comes at last
  To mingle with the sea."

And thus all night, above the wind,
  I heard the welcome rain,--
A fusillade upon the roof,
  A tattoo on the pane:
The key-hole piped; the chimney-top
  A warlike trumpet blew;
But, mingling with these sounds of strife,
  This hymn of peace stole through.

The Copperhead.

(1864.)

There is peace in the swamp where the Copper head sleeps,
Where the waters are stagnant, the white vapor creeps,
Where the musk of Magnolia hangs thick in the air,
And the lilies' phylacteries broaden in prayer;
There is peace in the swamp, though the quiet is Death,
Though the mist is miasm, the Upas tree's breath,
Though no echo awakes to the cooing of doves,--
There is peace: yes, the peace that the Copperhead loves!

Go seek him: he coils in the ooze and the drip
Like a thong idly flung from the slave-driver's whip;
But beware the false footstep,--the stumble that brings
A deadlier lash than the overseer swings.
Never arrow so true, never bullet so dread,
As the straight steady stroke of that hammershaped head;
Whether slave, or proud planter, who braves that dull crest,
Woe to him who shall trouble the Copperhead's rest!

Then why waste your labors, brave hearts and strong men,
In tracking a trail to the Copperhead's den?
Lay your axe to the cypress, hew open the shade
To the free sky and sunshine Jehovah has made;
Let the breeze of the North sweep the vapors away,
Till the stagnant lake ripples, the freed waters play;
And then to your heel can you righteously doom
The Copperhead born of its shadow and gloom!

On a Pen of Thomas Starr King.

This is the reed the dead musician dropped,
  With tuneful magic in its sheath still hidden;
The prompt allegro of its music stopped,
  Its melodies unbidden.

But who shall finish the unfinished strain,
  Or wake the instrument to awe and wonder,
And bid the slender barrel breathe again,--
  An organ-pipe of thunder?

His pen! what humbler memories cling about
  Its golden curves! what shapes and laughing graces
Slipped from its point, when his full heart went out
  In smiles and courtly phrases!

The truth, half jesting, half in earnest flung;
  The word of cheer, with recognition in it;
The note of alms, whose golden speech outrung
  The golden gift within it.

But all in vain the enchanter's wand we wave:
  No stroke of ours recalls his magic vision;
The incantation that its power gave
  Sleeps with the dead magician.

Lone Mountain.
(Cemetery, San Francisco.)

This is that hill of awe
That Persian Sindbad saw,--
  The mount magnetic;
And on its seaward face,
Scattered along its base,
  The wrecks prophetic.

Here come the argosies
Blown by each idle breeze,
  To and fro shifting;
Yet to the hill of Fate
All drawing, soon or late,--
  Day by day drifting;--

Drifting forever here
Barks that for many a year
  Braved wind and weather;
Shallops but yesterday
Launched on yon shining bay,--
  Drawn all together.

This is the end of all:
Sun thyself by the wall,
  O poorer Hindbad!
Envy not Sindbad's fame:
Here come alike the same,
  Hindbad and Sindbad.

California's Greeting to Seward.

(1869.)

We know him well: no need of praise
  Or bonfire from the windy hill
To light to softer paths and ways
  The world-worn man we honor still;

No need to quote those truths he spoke
  That burned through years of war and shame.
While History carves with surer stroke
  Across our map his noon-day fame;

No need to bid him show the scars
  Of blows dealt by the Scaean gate,
Who lived to pass its shattered bars,
  And see the foe capitulate;

Who lived to turn his slower feet
  Toward the western setting sun,
To see his harvest all complete,
  His dream fulfilled, his duty done,--

The one flag streaming from the pole,
  The one faith borne from sea to sea,--
For such a triumph, and such goal,
  Poor must our human greeting be.

Ah! rather that the conscious land
  In simpler ways salute the Man,--

The tall pines bowing where they stand,
  The bared head of El Capitan,

The tumult of the waterfalls,
  Pohono's kerchief in the breeze,
The waving from the rocky walls,
  The stir and rustle of the trees;

Till lapped in sunset skies of hope,
  In sunset lands by sunset seas,
The Young World's Premier treads the slope
  Of sunset years in calm and peace.

The Two Ships.

As I stand by the cross on the lone mountain's crest,
  Looking over the ultimate sea,
In the gloom of the mountain a ship lies at rest,
  And one sails away from the lea:
One spreads its white wings on a far-reaching track,
  With pennant and sheet flowing free;
One hides in the shadow with sails laid aback,--
  The ship that is waiting for me!

But lo, in the distance the clouds break away!
  The Gate's glowing portals I see;
And I hear from the outgoing ship in the bay
  The song of the sailors in glee.
So I think of the luminous footprints that bore

The comfort o'er dark Galilee,
And wait for the signal to go to the shore,
To the ship that is waiting for me.

The Goddess.
For the Sanitary Fair.

"Who comes?" The sentry's warning cry
  Rings sharply on the evening air:
Who comes? The challenge: no reply,
  Yet something motions there.

A woman, by those graceful folds;
  A soldier, by that martial tread:
"Advance three paces. Halt! until
  Thy name and rank be said."

"My name? Her name, in ancient song,
  Who fearless from Olympus came:
Look on me! Mortals know me best
  In battle and in flame."

"Enough! I know that clarion voice;
  I know that gleaming eye and helm;
Those crimson lips,--and in their dew
  The best blood of the realm.

"The young, the brave, the good and wise,

Have fallen in thy curst embrace:
The juices of the grapes of wrath
  Still stain thy guilty face.

"My brother lies in yonder field,
  Face downward to the quiet grass:
Go back! he cannot see thee now;
  But here thou shalt not pass."

A crack upon the evening air,
  A wakened echo from the hill:
The watch-dog on the distant shore
  Gives mouth, and all is still.

The sentry with his brother lies
  Face downward on the quiet grass;
And by him, in the pale moonshine,
  A shadow seems to pass.

No lance or warlike shield it bears:
  A helmet in its pitying hands
Brings water from the nearest brook,
  To meet his last demands.

Can this be she of haughty mien,
  The goddess of the sword and shield?
Ah, yes! The Grecian poet's myth
  Sways still each battle-field.

For not alone that rugged war
  Some grace or charm from beauty gains;
But, when the goddess' work is done,
  The woman's still remains.

Address.

Opening of the California Theatre, San Francisco, Jan. 19, 1870

Brief words, when actions wait, are well
The prompter's hand is on his bell;
The coming heroes, lovers, kings,
Are idly lounging at the wings;
Behind the curtain's mystic fold
The glowing future lies unrolled,--
And yet, one moment for the Past;
One retrospect,--the first and last.

"The world's a stage," the master said.
To-night a mightier truth is read:
Not in the shifting canvas screen,
The flash of gas, or tinsel sheen;
Not in the skill whose signal calls
From empty boards baronial halls;
But, fronting sea and curving bay,
Behold the players and the play.

Ah, friends! beneath your real skies
The actor's short-lived triumph dies:
On that broad stage, of empire won
Whose footlights were the setting sun,
Whose flats a distant background rose
In trackless peaks of endless snows;
Here genius bows, and talent waits
To copy that but One creates.

Your shifting scenes: the league of sand,
An avenue by ocean spanned;
The narrow beach of straggling tents,
A mile of stately monuments;
Your standard, lo! a flag unfurled,
Whose clinging folds clasp half the world,--
This is your drama, built on facts,
With "twenty years between the acts."

One moment more: if here we raise
The oft-sung hymn of local praise,
Before the curtain facts must sway;
Here waits the moral of your play.
Glassed in the poet's thought, you view
What ***money*** can, yet cannot do;
The faith that soars, the deeds that shine,
Above the gold that builds the shrine.

And oh! when others take our place,
And Earth's green curtain hides our face,
Ere on the stage, so silent now,
The last new hero makes his bow:
So may our deeds, recalled once more
In Memory's sweet but brief encore,
Down all the circling ages run,
With the world's plaudit of "Well done!"

The Lost Galleon.

In sixteen hundred and forty-one,
The regular yearly galleon,
Laden with odorous gums and spice,
India cottons and India rice,
And the richest silks of far Cathay,
Was due at Acapulco Bay.

Due she was, and over-due,--
Galleon, merchandise, and crew,
Creeping along through rain and shine,
Through the tropics, under the line.

The trains were waiting outside the walls,
The wives of sailors thronged the town,
The traders sat by their empty stalls,
And the viceroy himself came down;
The bells in the tower were all a-trip,
Te Deums were on each father's lip,
The limes were ripening in the sun
For the sick of the coming galleon.

All in vain. Weeks passed away,
And yet no galleon saw the bay:
India goods advanced in price;
The governor missed his favorite spice;
The senoritas mourned for sandal,
And the famous cottons of Coromandel;

And some for an absent lover lost,
And one for a husband,--Donna Julia,
Wife of the captain, tempest-tossed,
In circumstances so peculiar:
Even the fathers, unawares,
Grumbled a little at their prayers;
And all along the coast that year
Votive candles were scarce and dear.

Never a tear bedims the eye
That time and patience will not dry;
Never a lip is curved with pain
That can't be kissed into smiles again:
And these same truths, as far as I know,
Obtained on the coast of Mexico
More than two hundred years ago,

In sixteen hundred and fifty-one,--
Ten years after the deed was done,--
And folks had forgotten the galleon:
The divers plunged in the Gulf for pearls,
White as the teeth of the Indian girls;
The traders sat by their full bazaars;
The mules with many a weary load,
And oxen, dragging their creaking cars,
Came and went on the mountain road.

Where was the galleon all this while:
Wrecked on some lonely coral isle?
Burnt by the roving sea-marauders,
Or sailing north under secret orders?
Had she found the Anian passage famed,
By lying Moldonado claimed,

And sailed through the sixty-fifth degree
Direct to the North Atlantic sea?
Or had she found the "River of Kings,"
Of which De Fonte told such strange things
In sixteen forty? Never a sign,
East or West or under the line,
They saw of the missing galleon;
Never a sail or plank or chip,
They found of the long-lost treasure-ship,
Or enough to build a tale upon.
But when she was lost, and where and how,
Are the facts we're coming to just now.

Take, if you please, the chart of that day
Published at Madrid,--por el Rey;
Look for a spot in the old South Sea,
The hundred and eightieth degree
Longitude, west of Madrid: there,
Under the equatorial glare,
Just where the East and West are one,
You'll find the missing galleon,--
You'll find the "San Gregorio," yet
Riding the seas, with sails all set,
Fresh as upon the very day
She sailed from Acapulco Bay.

How did she get there? What strange spell
Kept her two hundred years so well,
Free from decay and mortal taint?
What? but the prayers of a patron saint!
A hundred leagues from Manilla town,
The "San Gregorio's" helm came down;
Round she went on her heel, and not

East and West

A cable's length from a galliot
That rocked on the waters, just abreast
Of the galleon's course, which was west-sou-west.

Then said the galleon's commandante,
General Pedro Sobriente
(That was his rank on land and main,
A regular custom of Old Spain),
"My pilot is dead of scurvy: may
I ask the longitude, time, and day?"
The first two given and compared;
The third,--the commandante stared!

"The *first* of June? I make it second."
Said the stranger, "Then you've wrongly-reckoned;
I make it *first*: as you came this way,
You should have lost--d'ye see--a day;
Lost a day, as plainly see,
On the hundred and eightieth degree."
"Lost a day?" "Yes: if not rude,
When did you make east longitude?"
"On the ninth of May,--our patron's day."
"On the ninth?--you had no ninth of May!
Eighth and tenth was there; but stay"--
Too late; for the galleon bore away.

Lost was the day they should have kept,
Lost unheeded and lost unwept;
Lost in a way that made search vain,
Lost in the trackless and boundless main;
Lost like the day of Job's awful curse,
In his third chapter, third and fourth verse;
Wrecked was their patron's only day,--

What would the holy fathers say?

Said the Fray Antonio Estavan,
The galleon's chaplain,--a learned man,--
"Nothing is lost that you can regain:
And the way to look for a thing is plain
To go where you lost it, back again.
Back with your galleon till you see
The hundred and eightieth degree.
Wait till the rolling year goes round,
And there will the missing day be found;
For you'll find--if computation's true--
That sailing *east* will give to you
Not only one ninth of May, but two,--
One for the good saint's present cheer,
And one for the day we lost last year."

Back to the spot sailed the galleon;
Where, for a twelve-month, off and on
The hundred and eightieth degree,
She rose and fell on a tropic sea:
But lo! when it came to the ninth of May,
All of a sudden becalmed she lay
One degree from that fatal spot,
Without the power to move a knot;
And of course the moment she lost her way,
Gone was her chance to save that day.

To cut a lengthening story short,
She never saved it. Made the sport
Of evil spirits and baffling wind,
She was always before or just behind,
One day too soon, or one day too late,

And the sun, meanwhile, would never wait:
She had two eighths, as she idly lay,
Two tenths, but never a *ninth* of May;
And there she rides through two hundred years
Of dreary penance and anxious fears:
Yet through the grace of the saint she served,
Captain and crew are still preserved.

By a computation that still holds good,
Made by the Holy Brotherhood,
The "San Gregorio" will cross that line
In nineteen hundred and thirty-nine:
Just three hundred years to a day
From the time she lost the ninth of May.
And the folk in Acapulco town,
Over the waters, looking down,
Will see in the glow of the setting sun
The sails of the missing galleon,
And the royal standard of Philip *Rey*;
The gleaming mast and glistening spar,
As she nears the surf of the outer bar.
A *Te Deum* sung on her crowded deck,
An odor of spice along the shore,
A crash, a cry from a shattered wreck,--
And the yearly galleon sails no more,
In or out of the olden bay;
For the blessed patron has found his day.

* * * * *

Such is the legend. Hear this truth:
Over the trackless past, somewhere,
Lie the lost days of our tropic youth,

Only regained by faith and prayer,
Only recalled by prayer and plaint:
Each lost day has its patron saint!

A Second Review of the Grand Army.

I read last night of the Grand Review
In Washington's chiefest avenue,--
Two Hundred Thousand men in blue,
  I think they said was the number,--
Till I seemed to hear their trampling feet,
The bugle blast and the drum's quick beat,
The clatter of hoofs in the stony street,
The cheers of people who came to greet,
And the thousand details that to repeat
  Would only my verse encumber,--
Till I fell in a reverie, sad and sweet,
  And then to a fitful slumber.

When, lo! in a vision I seemed to stand
In the lonely Capitol. On each hand
Far stretched the portico, dim and grand
Its columns ranged like a martial band
Of sheeted spectres, whom some command
  Had called to a last reviewing.
And the streets of the city were white and bare;
No footfall echoed across the square;
But out of the misty midnight air
I heard in the distance a trumpet blare,

And the wandering night-winds seemed to bear
  The sound of a far tattooing.

Then I held my breath with fear and dread;
For into the square, with a brazen tread,
There rode a figure whose stately head
  O'erlooked the review that morning,
That never bowed from its firm-set seat
When the living column passed its feet,
Yet now rode steadily up the street
  To the phantom bugle's warning:

Till it reached the Capitol square, and wheeled,
And there in the moonlight stood revealed
A well-known form that in State and field
  Had led our patriot sires;
Whose face was turned to the sleeping camp,
Afar through the river's fog and damp,
That showed no flicker, nor waning lamp,
  Nor wasted bivouac fires.

And I saw a phantom army come,
With never a sound of fife or drum,
But keeping time to a throbbing hum
  Of wailing and lamentation:
The martyred heroes of Malvern Hill,
Of Gettysburg and Chancellorsville,
The men whose wasted figures fill
    The patriot graves of the nation.

And there came the nameless dead,--the men
Who perished in fever swamp and fen,
The slowly-starved of the prison-pen;

And, marching beside the others,
Came the dusky martyrs of Pillow's fight,
With limbs enfranchised and bearing bright;
I thought--perhaps 'twas the pale moonlight--
   They looked as white as their brothers!

And so all night marched the Nation's dead
With never a banner above them spread,
Nor a badge, nor a motto brandished;
No mark--save the bare uncovered head
   Of the silent bronze Reviewer;
With never an arch save the vaulted sky;
With never a flower save those that lie
On the distant graves--for love could buy
   No gift that was purer or truer.

So all night long swept the strange array,
So all night long till the morning gray
I watched for one who had passed away,
   With a reverent awe and wonder,--
Till a blue cap waved in the lengthening line,
And I knew that one who was kin of mine
Had come; and I spake--and lo! that sign
   Awakened me from my slumber.

Part II.

Before the Curtain.

Behind the footlights hangs the rusty baize,
A trifle shabby in the upturned blaze
Of flaring gas, and curious eyes that gaze.

The stage, methinks, perhaps is none too wide,
And hardly fit for royal Richard's stride,
Or Falstaff's bulk, or Denmark's youthful pride.

Ah, well! no passion walks its humble boards;
O'er it no king nor valiant Hector lords:
The simplest skill is all its space affords.

The song and jest, the dance and trifling play,
The local hit at follies of the day,
The trick to pass an idle hour away,--

For these, no trumpets that announce the Moor,
No blast that makes the hero's welcome sure,--
A single fiddle in the overture!

The Stage-Driver's Story.

It was the stage-driver's story, as he stood with his back to the wheelers,
Quietly flecking his whip, and turning his quid of tobacco;
While on the dusty road, and blent with the rays of the moonlight,
We saw the long curl of his lash and the juice of tobacco descending.

"Danger! Sir, I believe you,--indeed, I may say on that subject,
You your existence might put to the hazard and turn of a wager.
I have seen danger? Oh, no! not me, sir, indeed, I assure you:
'Twas only the man with the dog that is sitting alone in yon wagon.

It was the Geiger Grade, a mile and a half from the summit:
Black as your hat was the night, and never a star in the heavens.
Thundering down the grade, the gravel and stones we sent flying
Over the precipice side,--a thousand feet plumb to the bottom.

Half-way down the grade I felt, sir, a thrilling and creaking,
Then a lurch to one side, as we hung on the bank of the canon;
Then, looking up the road, I saw, in the distance behind me,
The off hind wheel of the coach just loosed from its axle, and following.

One glance alone I gave, then gathered together my ribbons,
Shouted, and flung them, outspread, on the straining necks of my cattle;
Screamed at the top of my voice, and lashed the air in my frenzy,
While down the Geiger Grade, on **three** wheels, the vehicle thundered.

Speed was our only chance, when again came the ominous rattle:
Crack, and another wheel slipped away, and was lost in the darkness.

Two only now were left; yet such was our fearful momentum,
Upright, erect, and sustained on *two* wheels, the vehicle thundered.

As some huge boulder, unloosed from its rocky shelf on the mountain,
Drives before it the hare and the timorous squirrel, far-leaping,
So down the Geiger Grade rushed the Pioneer coach, and before it
Leaped the wild horses, and shrieked in advance of the danger impending.

But to be brief in my tale. Again, ere we came to the level,
Slipped from its axle a wheel; so that, to be plain in my statement,
A matter of twelve hundred yards or more, as the distance may be,
We travelled upon *one* wheel, until we drove up to the station.

Then, sir, we sank in a heap; but, picking myself from the ruins,
I heard a noise up the grade; and looking, I saw in the distance
The three wheels following still, like moons on the horizon whirling,
Till, circling, they gracefully sank on the road at the side of the
    station.

This is my story, sir; a trifle, indeed, I assure you.
Much more, perchance, might be said; but I hold him, of all men, most
    lightly
Who swerves from the truth in his tale--No, thank you--Well, since you
    are pressing,
Perhaps I don't care if I do: you may give me the same, Jim,--no sugar."

Aspiring Miss de Laine.
A Chemical Narrative.

Certain facts which serve to explain
The physical charms of Miss Addie De Laine,
Who, as the common reports obtain,
Surpassed in complexion the lily and rose;
With a very sweet mouth and a *retrousse* nose;
A figure like Hebe's, or that which revolves
In a milliner's window, and partially solves
That question which mentor and moralist pains,
If grace may exist *minus* feeling or brains.

Of course the young lady had beaux by the score,
All that she wanted,--what girl could ask more?
Lovers that sighed, and lovers that swore,
Lovers that danced, and lovers that played,
Men of profession, of leisure, and trade;
But one, who was destined to take the high part
Of holding that mythical treasure, her heart,--
This lover--the wonder and envy of town--
Was a practising chemist,--a fellow called Brown.

I might here remark that 'twas doubted by many,
In regard to the heart, if Miss Addie had any;
But no one could look in that eloquent face,
With its exquisite outline, and features of grace,
And mark, through the transparent skin, how the tide
Ebbed and flowed at the impulse of passion or pride,--
None could look, who believed in the blood's circulation

As argued by Harvey, but saw confirmation,
That here, at least, Nature had triumphed o'er art,
And, as far as complexion went, she had a heart.

But this, *par parenthesis*. Brown was the man
Preferred of all others to carry her fan,
Hook her glove, drape her shawl, and do all that a belle
May demand of the lover she wants to treat well.
Folks wondered and stared that a fellow called Brown--
Abstracted and solemn, in manner a clown,
Ill dressed, with a lingering smell of the shop--
Should appear as her escort at party or hop.
Some swore he had cooked up some villanous charm,
Or love philter, not in the regular Pharm--
Acopea, and thus, from pure *malis prepense*,
Had bewitched and bamboozled the young lady's sense;
Others thought, with more reason, the secret to lie
In a magical wash or indelible dye;
While Society, with its censorious eye
And judgment impartial, stood ready to damn
What wasn't improper as being a sham.

For a fortnight the townfolk had all been agog
With a party, the finest the season had seen,
To be given in honor of Miss Pollywog,
Who was just coming out as a belle of sixteen.
The guests were invited: but one night before,
A carriage drew up at the modest back-door
Of Brown's lab'ratory; and, full in the glare
Of a big purple bottle, some closely-veiled fair
Alighted and entered: to make matters plain,
Spite of veils and disguises,--'twas Addie De Laine.

As a bower for true love, 'twas hardly the one
That a lady would choose to be wooed in or won:
No odor of rose or sweet jessamine's sigh
Breathed a fragrance to hallow their pledge of troth by,
Nor the balm that exhales from the odorous thyme;
But the gaseous effusions of chloride of lime,
And salts, which your chemist delights to explain
As the base of the smell of the rose and the drain.
Think of this, O ye lovers of sweetness! and know
What you smell, when you snuff up Lubin or Pinaud.

I pass by the greetings, the transports and bliss,
Which, of course, duly followed a meeting like this,
And come down to business;--for such the intent
Of the lady who now o'er the crucible leant,
In the glow of a furnace of carbon and lime,
Like a fairy called up in the new pantomime;--
And give but her words as she coyly looked down,
In reply to the questioning glances of Brown:
"I am taking the drops, and am using the paste,
And the little, white powders that had a sweet taste,
Which you told me would brighten the glance of my eye,
And the depilatory, and also the dye,
And I'm charmed with the trial; and now, my dear Brown,
I have one other favor,--now, ducky, don't frown,--
Only one, for a chemist and genius like you
But a trifle, and one you can easily do.
Now listen: tomorrow, you know, is the night
Of the birthday *soiree* of that Pollywog fright;
And I'm to be there, and the dress I shall wear
Is *too* lovely; but"--"But what then, *ma chere*?"
Said Brown, as the lady came to a full stop,
And glanced round the shelves of the little back shop.

"Well, I want--I want something to fill out the skirt
To the proper dimension, without being girt
In a stiff crinoline, or caged in a hoop
That shows through one's skirt like the bars of a coop;
Something light, that a lady may waltz in, or polk,
With a freedom that none but you masculine folk
Ever know. For, however poor woman aspires,
She's always bound down to the earth by these wires.
Are you listening? nonsense! don't stare like a spoon,
Idiotic; some light thing, and spacious, and soon--
Something like--well, in fact--something like a balloon!"
Here she paused; and here Brown, overcome by surprise,
Gave a doubting assent with still wondering eyes,
And the lady departed. But just at the door
Something happened,--'tis true, it had happened before
In this sanctum of science,--a sibilant sound,
Like some element just from its trammels unbound,
Or two substances that their affinities found.

The night of the anxiously looked-for *soiree*
Had come, with its fair ones in gorgeous array;
With the rattle of wheels, and the tinkle of bells,
And the "How do ye dos," and the "Hope you are wells;"
And the crash in the passage, and last lingering look
You give as you hang your best hat on the hook;
The rush of hot air as the door opens wide;
And your entry,--that blending of self-possessed pride
And humility shown in your perfect-bred stare
At the folk, as if wondering how they got there;
With other tricks worthy of Vanity Fair.
Meanwhile that safe topic, the heat of the room,
Already was losing its freshness and bloom;
Young people were yawning, and wondering when

The dance would come off, and why didn't it then:
When a vague expectation was thrilling the crowd,
Lo, the door swung its hinges with utterance proud!
And Pompey announced, with a trumpet-like strain,
The entrance of Brown and Miss Addie De Laine.

She entered: but oh, how imperfect the verb
To express to the senses her movement superb!
To say that she "sailed in" more clearly might tell
Her grace in its buoyant and billowy swell.
Her robe was a vague circumambient space,
With shadowy boundaries made of point-lace.
The rest was but guess-work, and well might defy
The power of critical feminine eye
To define or describe: 'twere as futile to try
The gossamer web of the cirrus to trace,
Floating far in the blue of a warm summer sky.

'Midst the humming of praises and the glances of beaux,
That greet our fair maiden wherever she goes,
Brown slipped like a shadow, grim, silent, and black,
With a look of anxiety, close in her track.
Once he whispered aside in her delicate ear,
A sentence of warning,--it might be of fear:
"Don't stand in a draught, if you value your life."
(Nothing more,--such advice might be given your wife
Or your sweetheart, in times of bronchitis and cough,
Without mystery, romance, or frivolous scoff.)
But hark to the music: the dance has begun.
The closely-draped windows wide open are flung;
The notes of the piccolo, joyous and light,
Like bubbles burst forth on the warm summer night.
Round about go the dancers; in circles they fly;

Trip, trip, go their feet as their skirts eddy by;
And swifter and lighter, but somewhat too plain,
Whisks the fair circumvolving Miss Addie De Laine.

Taglioni and Cerito well might have pined
For the vigor and ease that her movements combined;
E'en Rigelboche never flung higher her robe
In the naughtiest city that's known on the globe.
'Twas amazing, 'twas scandalous: lost in surprise,
Some opened their mouths, and a few shut their eyes.

But hark! At the moment Miss Addie De Laine,
Circling round at the outer edge of an ellipse,
Which brought her fair form to the window again,
From the arms of her partner incautiously slips!
And a shriek fills the air, and the music is still,
And the crowd gather round where her partner forlorn
Still frenziedly points from the wide window-sill
Into space and the night; for Miss Addie was gone!

Gone like the bubble that bursts in the sun;
Gone like the grain when the reaper is done;
Gone like the dew on the fresh morning grass;
Gone without parting farewell; and alas!
Gone with a flavor of Hydrogen Gas.

When the weather is pleasant, you frequently meet
A white-headed man slowly pacing the street;
His trembling hand shading his lack-lustre eye,
Half blind with continually scanning the sky.

Rumor points him as some astronomical sage,
Reperusing by day the celestial page;

But the reader, sagacious, will recognize Brown,
Trying vainly to conjure his lost sweetheart down,
And learn the stern moral this story must teach,
That Genius may lift its love out of its reach.

California Madrigal.
On the Approach of Spring.

Oh come, my beloved! from thy winter abode,
From thy home on the Yuba, thy ranch overflowed;
For the waters have fallen, the winter has fled,
And the river once more has returned to its bed.

Oh, mark how the spring in its beauty is near!
How the fences and tules once more re-appear!
How soft lies the mud on the banks of yon slough
By the hole in the levee the waters broke through!

All Nature, dear Chloris, is blooming to greet
The glance of your eye, and the tread of your feet;
For the trails are all open, the roads are all free,
And the highwayman's whistle is heard on the lea.

Again swings the lash on the high mountain trail,
And the pipe of the packer is scenting the gale;
The oath and the jest ringing high o'er the plain,
Where the smut is not always confined to the grain.

Once more glares the sunlight on awning and roof,
Once more the red clay's pulverized by the hoof,
Once more the dust powders the "outsides" with red,
Once more at the station the whiskey is spread.

Then fly with me, love, ere the summer's begun,
And the mercury mounts to one hundred and one;
Ere the grass now so green shall be withered and sear,
In the spring that obtains but one month in the year.

St. Thomas.
A Geographical Survey.

(1868.)

Very fair and full of promise
Lay the island of St. Thomas:
Ocean o'er its reefs and bars
Hid its elemental scars;
Groves of cocoanut and guava
Grew above its fields of lava.
So the gem of the Antilles,--
"Isles of Eden," where no ill is,--
Like a great green turtle slumbered
On the sea that it encumbered.
Then said William Henry Seward,
As he cast his eye to leeward,
"Quite important to our commerce

Is this island of St. Thomas."

Said the Mountain ranges, "Thank'ee,
But we cannot stand the Yankee
O'er our scars and fissures poring,
In our very vitals boring,
In our sacred caverns prying,
All our secret problems trying,--
Digging, blasting, with dynamit
Mocking all our thunders! Damn it!
Other lands may be more civil,
Bust our lava crust if we will."

Said the Sea,--its white teeth gnashing
Through its coral-reef lips flashing,--
"Shall I let this scheming mortal
Shut with stone my shining portal,
Curb my tide, and check my play,
Fence with wharves my shining bay?
Rather let me be drawn out
In one awful water-spout!"

Said the black-browed Hurricane,
Brooding down the Spanish main,
"Shall I see my forces, zounds!
Measured by square inch and pounds,
With detectives at my back
When I double on my track,
And my secret paths made clear,
Published o'er the hemisphere
To each gaping, prying crew?
Shall I? Blow me if I do!"

So the Mountains shook and thundered,
And the Hurricane came sweeping,
And the people stared and wondered
As the Sea came on them leaping:
Each, according to his promise,
Made things lively at St. Thomas.

Till one morn, when Mr. Seward
Cast his weather eye to leeward,
There was not an inch of dry land
Left to mark his recent island.

Not a flagstaff or a sentry,
Not a wharf or port of entry,--
Only--to cut matters shorter--
Just a patch of muddy water
In the open ocean lying,
And a gull above it flying.

The Ballad of Mr. Cooke.
A Legend of the Cliff House, San Francisco.

Where the sturdy ocean breeze
Drives the spray of roaring seas
That the Cliff-House balconies
      Overlook:

There, in spite of rain that balked,
With his sandals duly chalked,
Once upon a tight-rope walked
      Mr. Cooke.

But the jester's lightsome mien,
And his spangles and his sheen,
All had vanished, when the scene
      He forsook;----

Yet in some delusive hope,
In some vague desire to cope,
One still came to view the rope
      Walked by Cooke.

Amid Beauty's bright array,
On that strange eventful day,
Partly hidden from the spray,
      In a nook,

Stood Florinda Vere de Vere;
Who with wind-dishevelled hair,

And a rapt, distracted air,
        Gazed on Cooke.

Then she turned, and quickly cried
To her lover at her side,
While her form with love and pride
        Wildly shook,

"Clifford Snook! oh, hear me now!
Here I break each plighted vow:
There's but one to whom I bow,
        And that's Cooke!"

Haughtily that young man spoke:
"I descend from noble folk.
'Seven Oaks,' and then 'Se'nnoak,'
        Lastly Snook,

Is the way my name I trace:
Shall a youth of noble race
In affairs of love give place
        To a Cooke?"

"Clifford Snook, I know thy claim
To that lineage and name,
And I think I've read the same
        In Horne Tooke;

But I swear, by all divine,
Never, never to be thine,
'Till thou canst upon yon line
        Walk like Cooke."

Though to that gymnastic feat
He no closer might compete
Than to strike a **balance**-sheet
        In a book;

Yet thenceforward, from that day,
He his figure would display
In some wild athletic way,
        After Cooke.

On some household eminence,
On a clothes-line or a fence,
Over ditches, drains, and thence
        O'er a brook,

He, by high ambition led,
Ever walked and balanced;
Till the people, wondering, said,
        "How like Cooke!"

Step by step did he proceed,
Nerved by valor, not by greed,
And at last the crowning deed
        Undertook:

Misty was the midnight air,
And the cliff was bleak and bare,
When he came to do and dare
        Just like Cooke.

Through the darkness, o'er the flow,
Stretched the line where he should go
Straight across, as flies the crow

            Or the rook:

One wild glance around he cast;
Then he faced the ocean blast,
And he strode the cable last
            Touched by Cooke.

Vainly roared the angry seas;
Vainly blew the ocean breeze;
But, alas! the walker's knees
            Had a crook;

And before he reached the rock
Did they both together knock,
And he stumbled with a shock--
            Unlike Cooke!

Downward dropping in the dark,
Like an arrow to its mark,
Or a fish-pole when a shark
            Bites the hook,

Dropped the pole he could not save,
Dropped the walker, and the wave
Swift ingulfed the rival brave
            Of J. Cooke!

Came a roar across the sea
Of sea-lions in their glee,
In a tongue remarkably
            Like Chinnook;

And the maddened sea-gull seemed
Still to utter, as he screamed,
"Perish thus the wretch who deemed
      Himself Cooke!"

But, on misty moonlit nights,
Comes a skeleton in tights,
Walks once more the giddy heights
      He mistook;

And unseen to mortal eyes,
Purged of grosser earthly ties,
Now at last in spirit guise
      Outdoes Cooke.

Still the sturdy ocean breeze
Sweeps the spray of roaring seas,
Where the Cliff-House balconies
      Overlook;

And the maidens in their prime,
Reading of this mournful rhyme,
Weep where, in the olden time,
      Walked J. Cooke.

The Legends of the Rhine.

Beetling walls with ivy grown,
Frowning heights of mossy stone;
Turret, with its flaunting flag
Flung from battlemented crag;
Dungeon-keep and fortalice
Looking down a precipice
O'er the darkly glancing wave
By the Lurline-haunted cave;
Robber haunt and maiden bower,
Home of Love and Crime and Power,--
That's the scenery, in fine,
Of the Legends of the Rhine.

One bold baron, double-dyed
Bigamist and parricide,
And, as most the stories run,
Partner of the Evil One;
Injured innocence in white,
Fair but idiotic quite,
Wringing of her lily hands;
Valor fresh from Paynim lands,
Abbot ruddy, hermit pale,
Minstrel fraught with many a tale,--
Are the actors that combine
In the Legends of the Rhine.

Bell-mouthed flagons round a board;
Suits of armor, shield, and sword;
Kerchief with its bloody stain;

Ghosts of the untimely slain;
Thunder-clap and clanking chain;
Headsman's block and shining axe;
Thumbscrews, crucifixes, racks;
Midnight-tolling chapel bell,
Heard across the gloomy fell,--
These, and other pleasant facts,
Are the properties that shine
In the Legends of the Rhine.

Maledictions, whispered vows
Underneath the linden boughs;
Murder, bigamy, and theft;
Travellers of goods bereft;
Rapine, pillage, arson, spoil,--
Every thing but honest toil,
Are the deeds that best define
Every Legend of the Rhine.

That Virtue always meets reward,
But quicker when it wears a sword;
That Providence has special care
Of gallant knight and lady fair;
That villains, as a thing of course,
Are always haunted by remorse,--
Is the moral, I opine,
Of the Legends of the Rhine.

Mrs. Judge Jenkins.

[Being the Only Genuine Sequel to "Maud Muller."]

Maud Muller, all that summer day,
Raked the meadow sweet with hay;

Yet, looking down the distant lane,
She hoped the judge would come again.

But when he came, with smile and bow,
Maud only blushed, and stammered, "Ha-ow?"

And spoke of her "pa," and wondered whether
He'd give consent they should wed together.

Old Muller burst in tears, and then
Begged that the judge would lend him "ten;"

For trade was dull, and wages low,
And the "craps," this year, were somewhat slow.

And ere the languid summer died,
Sweet Maud became the judge's bride.

But, on the day that they were mated,
Maud's brother Bob was intoxicated;

And Maud's relations, twelve in all,
Were very drunk at the judge's hall.

And when the summer came again,
The young bride bore him babies twain.

And the judge was blest, but thought it strange
That bearing children made such a change:

For Maud grew broad and red and stout;
And the waist that his arm once clasped about

Was more than he now could span. And he
Sighed as he pondered, ruefully,

How that which in Maud was native grace
In Mrs. Jenkins was out of place;

And thought of the twins, and wished that they
Looked less like the man who raked the hay

On Muller's farm, and dreamed with pain
Of the day he wandered down the lane.

And, looking down that dreary track,
He half regretted that he came back.

For, had he waited, he might have wed
Some maiden fair and thoroughbred;

For there be women fair as she,
Whose verbs and nouns do more agree.

Alas for maiden! alas for judge!
And the sentimental,--that's one-half "fudge;"

For Maud soon thought the judge a bore,
With all his learning and all his lore.

And the judge would have bartered Maud's fair face
For more refinement and social grace.

If, of all words of tongue and pen,
The saddest are, "It might have been,"

More sad are these we daily see:
"It is, but hadn't ought to be."

Avitor.
An Aerial Retrospect.

What was it filled my youthful dreams,
In place of Greek or Latin themes,
Or beauty's wild, bewildering beams?
        Avitor?

What visions and celestial scenes
I filled with aerial machines,--
Montgolfier's and Mr. Green's!
        Avitor.

What fairy tales seemed things of course!
The rock that brought Sindbad across,
The Calendar's own winged-horse!
        Avitor!

How many things I took for facts,--
Icarus and his conduct lax,
And how he sealed his fate with wax!
   Avitor!

The first balloons I sought to sail,
Soap-bubbles fair, but all too frail,
Or kites,--but thereby hangs a tail.
   Avitor!

What made me launch from attic tall
A kitten and a parasol,
And watch their bitter, frightful fall?
   Avitor?

What youthful dreams of high renown
Bade me inflate the parson's gown,
That went not up, nor yet came down?
   Avitor?

My first ascent, I may not tell:
Enough to know that in that well
My first high aspirations fell,
   Avitor!

My other failures let me pass:
The dire explosions; and, alas!
The friends I choked with noxious gas,
   Avitor!
For lo! I see perfected rise
The vision of my boyish eyes,
The messenger of upper skies,
   Avitor!

A White-Pine Ballad.

Recently with Samuel Johnson this occasion I improved,
Whereby certain gents of affluence I hear were greatly moved;
But not all of Johnson's folly, although multiplied by nine,
Could compare with Milton Perkins, late an owner in White Pine.

Johnson's folly--to be candid--was a wild desire to treat
Every able male white citizen he met upon the street;
And there being several thousand--but this subject why pursue?
'Tis with Perkins, and not Johnson, that to-day we have to do.

No: not wild promiscuous treating, not the winecup's ruby flow,
But the female of his species brought the noble Perkins low.
'Twas a wild poetic fervor, and excess of sentiment,
That left the noble Perkins in a week without a cent.

"Milton Perkins," said the Siren, "not thy wealth do I admire,
But the intellect that flashes from those eyes of opal fire;
And methinks the name thou bearest surely cannot be misplaced,
And, embrace me, Mister Perkins!" Milton Perkins her embraced.

But I grieve to state, that even then, as she was wiping dry
The tear of sensibility in Milton Perkins' eye,
She prigged his diamond bosom-pin, and that her wipe of lace
Did seem to have of chloroform a most suspicious trace.

Enough that Milton Perkins later in the night was found
With his head in an ash-barrel, and his feet upon the ground;
And he murmured "Seraphina," and he kissed his hand, and smiled
On a party who went through him, like an unresisting child.

Moral.

Now one word to Pogonippers, ere this subject I resign,
In this tale of Milton Perkins,--late an owner in White Pine,--
You shall see that wealth and women are deceitful, just the same;
And the tear of sensibility has salted many a claim.

What the Wolf Really Said to Little Red Riding-Hood.

Wondering maiden, so puzzled and fair,
Why dost thou murmur and ponder and stare?
"Why are my eyelids so open and wild?"--
Only the better to see with, my child!
Only the better and clearer to view
Cheeks that are rosy, and eyes that are blue.

Dost thou still wonder, and ask why these arms
Fill thy soft bosom with tender alarms,
Swaying so wickedly?--are they misplaced,
Clasping or shielding some delicate waist:
Hands whose coarse sinews may fill you with fear
Only the better protect you, my dear!

Little Red Riding-Hood, when in the street,
Why do I press your small hand when we meet?
Why, when you timidly offered your cheek,
Why did I sigh, and why didn't I speak?

Why, well: you see--if the truth must appear--
I'm not your grandmother, Riding-Hood, dear!

The Ritualist.
By a Communicant of "St. James's."

He wore, I think, a chasuble, the day when first we met;
A stole and snowy alb likewise: I recollect it yet.
He called me "daughter," as he raised his jewelled hand to bless;
And then, in thrilling undertones, he asked, "Would I confess?"

O mother, dear! blame not your child, if then on bended knees
I dropped, and thought of Abelard, and also Eloise;
Or when, beside the altar high, he bowed before the pyx,
I envied that seraphic kiss he gave the crucifix.

The cruel world may think it wrong, perhaps may deem me weak,
And, speaking of that sainted man, may call his conduct "cheek;"
And, like that wicked barrister whom Cousin Harry quotes,
May term his mixed chalice "grog," his vestments, "petticoats."

But, whatsoe'er they do or say, I'll build a Christian's hope
On incense and on altar-lights, on chasuble and cope.
Let others prove, by precedent, the faith that they profess:
"His can't be wrong" that's symbolized by such becoming dress.

A Moral Vindicator.

If Mr. Jones, Lycurgus B.,
Had one peculiar quality,
'Twas his severe advocacy
Of conjugal fidelity.

His views of heaven were very free;
His views of life were painfully
Ridiculous; but fervently
He dwelt on marriage sanctity.

He frequently went on a spree;
But in his wildest revelry,
On this especial subject he
Betrayed no ambiguity.

And though at times Lycurgus B.
Did lay his hands not lovingly
Upon his wife, the sanctity
Of wedlock was his guaranty.

But Mrs. Jones declined to see
Affairs in the same light as he,
And quietly got a decree
Divorcing her from that L. B.

And what did Jones, Lycurgus B.,
With his known idiosyncrasy?
He smiled,--a bitter smile to see,--
And drew the weapon of Bowie.

He did what Sickles did to Key,--
What Cole on Hiscock wrought, did he;
In fact, on persons twenty-three
He proved the marriage sanctity.

The counsellor who took the fee,
The witnesses and referee,
The judge who granted the decree,
Died in that wholesale butchery.

And then when Jones, Lycurgus B.,
Had wiped the weapon of Bowie,
Twelve jurymen did instantly
Acquit and set Lycurgus free.

Songs Without Sense.
For the Parlor and Piano.

I.--The Personified Sentimental.

Affection's charm no longer gilds
  The idol of the shrine;
But cold Oblivion seeks to fill
  Regret's ambrosial wine.
Though Friendship's offering buried lies
  'Neath cold Aversion's snow,
Regard and Faith will ever bloom
  Perpetually below.

I see thee whirl in marble halls,
  In Pleasure's giddy train;
Remorse is never on that brow,
  Nor Sorrow's mark of pain.
Deceit has marked thee for her own;
  Inconstancy the same;
And Ruin wildly sheds its gleam
  Athwart thy path of shame.

II.--The Homely Pathetic.

The dews are heavy on my brow;
  My breath comes hard and low;
Yet, mother, dear, grant one request,
  Before your boy must go.
Oh! lift me ere my spirit sinks,
  And ere my senses fail:
Place me once more, O mother dear!
  Astride the old fence-rail.

The old fence-rail, the old fence-rail!
  How oft these youthful legs,
With Alice' and Ben Bolt's, were hung
  Across those wooden pegs.
'Twas there the nauseating smoke
  Of my first pipe arose:
O mother, dear! these agonies
  Are far less keen than those.

I know where lies the hazel dell,
  Where simple Nellie sleeps;
I know the cot of Nettie Moore,
  And where the willow weeps.
I know the brookside and the mill:
  But all their pathos fails
Beside the days when once I sat
  Astride the old fence-rails.

III.--Swiss Air.

I'm a gay tra, la, la,
With my fal, lal, la, la,
And my bright--
And my light--
  Tra, la, le. [Repeat.]

Then laugh, ha, ha, ha,
And ring, ting, ling, ling,
And sing fal, la, la,
  La, la, le. [Repeat.]

www.bookjungle.com *email: sales@bookjungle.com fax: 630-214-0564 mail: Book Jungle PO Box 2226 Champaign, IL 61825*

The Codes Of Hammurabi And Moses
W. W. Davies

QTY

The discovery of the Hammurabi Code is one of the greatest achievements of archaeology, and is of paramount interest, not only to the student of the Bible, but also to all those interested in ancient history...

Religion   **ISBN:** *1-59462-338-4*   **Pages:132**
MSRP $12.95

The Theory of Moral Sentiments
Adam Smith

QTY

This work from 1749. contains original theories of conscience amd moral judgment and it is the foundation for systemof morals.

Philosophy ISBN: *1-59462-777-0*   **Pages:536**
MSRP $19.95

Jessica's First Prayer
Hesba Stretton

QTY

In a screened and secluded corner of one of the many railway-bridges which span the streets of London there could be seen a few years ago, from five o'clock every morning until half past eight, a tidily set-out coffee-stall, consisting of a trestle and board, upon which stood two large tin cans, with a small fire of charcoal burning under each so as to keep the coffee boiling during the early hours of the morning when the work-people were thronging into the city on their way to their daily toil...

Childrens   ISBN: *1-59462-373-2*   **Pages:84**
MSRP $9.95

My Life and Work
Henry Ford

QTY

Henry Ford revolutionized the world with his implementation of mass production for the Model T automobile. Gain valuable business insight into his life and work with his own auto-biography... "We have only started on our development of our country we have not as yet, with all our talk of wonderful progress, done more than scratch the surface. The progress has been wonderful enough but..."

Biographies/   ISBN: *1-59462-198-5*   **Pages:300**
MSRP $21.95

www.bookjungle.com email: sales@bookjungle.com fax: 630-214-0564 mail: Book Jungle PO Box 2226 Champaign, IL 61825

The Art of Cross-Examination
Francis Wellman

QTY

I presume it is the experience of every author, after his first book is published upon an important subject, to be almost overwhelmed with a wealth of ideas and illustrations which could readily have been included in his book, and which to his own mind, at least, seem to make a second edition inevitable. Such certainly was the case with me; and when the first edition had reached its sixth impression in five months, I rejoiced to learn that it seemed to my publishers that the book had met with a sufficiently favorable reception to justify a second and considerably enlarged edition. ...

Reference   ISBN: *1-59462-647-2*   Pages:412   MSRP *$19.95*

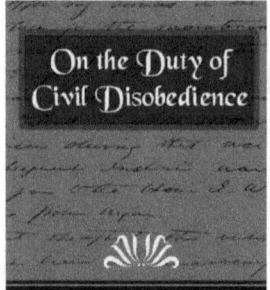

On the Duty of Civil Disobedience
Henry David Thoreau

QTY

Thoreau wrote his famous essay, On the Duty of Civil Disobedience, as a protest against an unjust but popular war and the immoral but popular institution of slave-owning. He did more than write—he declined to pay his taxes, and was hauled off to gaol in consequence. Who can say how much this refusal of his hastened the end of the war and of slavery ?

Law   ISBN: *1-59462-747-9*   Pages:48   MSRP *$7.45*

Dream Psychology Psychoanalysis for Beginners
Sigmund Freud

QTY

Sigmund Freud, born Sigismund Schlomo Freud (May 6, 1856 - September 23, 1939), was a Jewish-Austrian neurologist and psychiatrist who co-founded the psychoanalytic school of psychology. Freud is best known for his theories of the unconscious mind, especially involving the mechanism of repression; his redefinition of sexual desire as mobile and directed towards a wide variety of objects; and his therapeutic techniques, especially his understanding of transference in the therapeutic relationship and the presumed value of dreams as sources of insight into unconscious desires.

Psychology   ISBN: *1-59462-905-6*   Pages:196   MSRP *$15.45*

The Miracle of Right Thought
Orison Swett Marden

QTY

Believe with all of your heart that you will do what you were made to do. When the mind has once formed the habit of holding cheerful, happy, prosperous pictures, it will not be easy to form the opposite habit. It does not matter how improbable or how far away this realization may see, or how dark the prospects may be, if we visualize them as best we can, as vividly as possible, hold tenaciously to them and vigorously struggle to attain them, they will gradually become actualized, realized in the life. But a desire, a longing without endeavor, a yearning abandoned or held indifferently will vanish without realization.

Self Help   ISBN: *1-59462-644-8*   Pages:360   MSRP *$25.45*

www.bookjungle.com email: sales@bookjungle.com fax: 630-214-0564 mail: Book Jungle PO Box 2226 Champaign, IL 61825

QTY

☐ **The Rosicrucian Cosmo-Conception Mystic Christianity** by *Max Heindel* ISBN: *1-59462-188-8* **$38.95**
The Rosicrucian Cosmo-conception is not dogmatic, neither does it appeal to any other authority than the reason of the student. It is: not controversial, but is: sent forth in the, hope that it may help to clear...   New Age/Religion Pages 646

☐ **Abandonment To Divine Providence** by *Jean-Pierre de Caussade* ISBN: *1-59462-228-0* **$25.95**
"The Rev. Jean Pierre de Caussade was one of the most remarkable spiritual writers of the Society of Jesus in France in the 18th Century. His death took place at Toulouse in 1751. His works have gone through many editions and have been republished...   Inspirational/Religion Pages 400

☐ **Mental Chemistry** by *Charles Haanel* ISBN: *1-59462-192-6* **$23.95**
Mental Chemistry allows the change of material conditions by combining and appropriately utilizing the power of the mind. Much like applied chemistry creates something new and unique out of careful combinations of chemicals the mastery of mental chemistry...   New Age Pages 354

☐ **The Letters of Robert Browning and Elizabeth Barret Barrett 1845-1846 vol II** ISBN: *1-59462-193-4* **$35.95**
by *Robert Browning* and *Elizabeth Barrett*   Biographies Pages 596

☐ **Gleanings In Genesis (volume I)** by *Arthur W. Pink* ISBN: *1-59462-130-6* **$27.45**
Appropriately has Genesis been termed "the seed plot of the Bible" for in it we have, in germ form, almost all of the great doctrines which are afterwards fully developed in the books of Scripture which follow...   Religion/Inspirational Pages 420

☐ **The Master Key** by *L. W. de Laurence* ISBN: *1-59462-001-6* **$30.95**
In no branch of human knowledge has there been a more lively increase of the spirit of research during the past few years than in the study of Psychology, Concentration and Mental Discipline. The requests for authentic lessons in Thought Control, Mental Discipline and...   New Age/Business Pages 422

☐ **The Lesser Key Of Solomon Goetia** by *L. W. de Laurence* ISBN: *1-59462-092-X* **$9.95**
This translation of the first book of the "Lemegton" which is now for the first time made accessible to students of Talismanic Magic was done, after careful collation and edition, from numerous Ancient Manuscripts in Hebrew, Latin, and French...   New Age/Occult Pages 92

☐ **Rubaiyat Of Omar Khayyam** by *Edward Fitzgerald* ISBN:*1-59462-332-5* **$13.95**
Edward Fitzgerald, whom the world has already learned, in spite of his own efforts to remain within the shadow of anonymity, to look upon as one of the rarest poets of the century, was born at Bredfield, in Suffolk, on the 31st of March, 1809. He was the third son of John Purcell...   Music Pages 172

☐ **Ancient Law** by *Henry Maine* ISBN: *1-59462-128-4* **$29.95**
The chief object of the following pages is to indicate some of the earliest ideas of mankind, as they are reflected in Ancient Law, and to point out the relation of those ideas to modern thought.   Religion/History Pages 452

☐ **Far-Away Stories** by *William J. Locke* ISBN: *1-59462-129-2* **$19.45**
"Good wine needs no bush, but a collection of mixed vintages does. And this book is just such a collection. Some of the stories I do not want to remain buried for ever in the museum files of dead magazine-numbers an author's not unpardonable vanity..."   Fiction Pages 272

☐ **Life of David Crockett** by *David Crockett* ISBN: *1-59462-250-7* **$27.45**
"Colonel David Crockett was one of the most remarkable men of the times in which he lived. Born in humble life, but gifted with a strong will, an indomitable courage, and unremitting perseverance...   Biographies/New Age Pages 424

☐ **Lip-Reading** by *Edward Nitchie* ISBN: *1-59462-206-X* **$25.95**
Edward B. Nitchie, founder of the New York School for the Hard of Hearing, now the Nitchie School of Lip-Reading, Inc, wrote "LIP-READING Principles and Practice". The development and perfecting of this meritorious work on lip-reading was an undertaking...   How-to Pages 400

☐ **A Handbook of Suggestive Therapeutics, Applied Hypnotism, Psychic Science** ISBN: *1-59462-214-0* **$24.95**
by *Henry Munro*   Health/New Age/Health/Self-help Pages 376

☐ **A Doll's House: and Two Other Plays** by *Henrik Ibsen* ISBN: *1-59462-112-8* **$19.95**
Henrik Ibsen created this classic when in revolutionary 1848 Rome. Introducing some striking concepts in playwriting for the realist genre, this play has been studied the world over.   Fiction/Classics/Plays 308

☐ **The Light of Asia** by *sir Edwin Arnold* ISBN: *1-59462-204-3* **$13.95**
In this poetic masterpiece, Edwin Arnold describes the life and teachings of Buddha. The man who was to become known as Buddha to the world was born as Prince Gautama of India but he rejected the worldly riches and abandoned the reigns of power when...   Religion/History/Biographies Pages 170

☐ **The Complete Works of Guy de Maupassant** by *Guy de Maupassant* ISBN: *1-59462-157-8* **$16.95**
"For days and days, nights and nights, I had dreamed of that first kiss which was to consecrate our engagement, and I knew not on what spot I should put my lips..."   Fiction/Classics Pages 240

☐ **The Art of Cross-Examination** by *Francis L. Wellman* ISBN: *1-59462-309-0* **$26.95**
Written by a renowned trial lawyer, Wellman imparts his experience and uses case studies to explain how to use psychology to extract desired information through questioning.   How-to/Science/Reference Pages 408

☐ **Answered or Unanswered?** by *Louisa Vaughan* ISBN: *1-59462-248-5* **$10.95**
Miracles of Faith in China   Religion Pages 112

☐ **The Edinburgh Lectures on Mental Science (1909)** by *Thomas* ISBN: *1-59462-008-3* **$11.95**
This book contains the substance of a course of lectures recently given by the writer in the Queen Street Hall, Edinburgh. Its purpose is to indicate the Natural Principles governing the relation between Mental Action and Material Conditions...   New Age/Psychology Pages 148

☐ **Ayesha** by *H. Rider Haggard* ISBN: *1-59462-301-5* **$24.95**
Verily and indeed it is the unexpected that happens! Probably if there was one person upon the earth from whom the Editor of this, and of a certain previous history, did not expect to hear again...   Classics Pages 380

☐ **Ayala's Angel** by *Anthony Trollope* ISBN: *1-59462-352-X* **$29.95**
The two girls were both pretty, but Lucy who was twenty-one who supposed to be simple and comparatively unattractive, whereas Ayala was credited, as her Bombwhat romantic name might show, with poetic charm and a taste for romance. Ayala when her father died was nineteen...   Fiction Pages 484

☐ **The American Commonwealth** by *James Bryce* ISBN: *1-59462-286-8* **$34.45**
An interpretation of American democratic political theory. It examines political mechanics and society from the perspective of Scotsman James Bryce   Politics Pages 572

☐ **Stories of the Pilgrims** by *Margaret P. Pumphrey* ISBN: *1-59462-116-0* **$17.95**
This book explores pilgrims religious oppression in England as well as their escape to Holland and eventual crossing to America on the Mayflower, and their early days in New England...   History Pages 268

www.bookjungle.com email: sales@bookjungle.com fax: 630-214-0564 mail: Book Jungle PO Box 2226 Champaign, IL 61825

QTY

The Fasting Cure *by Sinclair Upton*   ISBN: *1-59462-222-1*   **$13.95**
In the Cosmopolitan Magazine for May, 1910, and in the Contemporary Review (London) for April, 1910, I published an article dealing with my experiences in fasting. I have written a great many magazine articles, but never one which attracted so much attention...   New Age/Self Help/Health Pages 164

Hebrew Astrology *by Sepharial*   ISBN: *1-59462-308-2*   **$13.45**
In these days of advanced thinking it is a matter of common observation that we have left many of the old landmarks behind and that we are now pressing forward to greater heights and to a wider horizon than that which represented the mind-content of our progenitors...   Astrology Pages 144

Thought Vibration or The Law of Attraction in the Thought World   ISBN: *1-59462-127-6*   **$12.95**
by William Walker Atkinson   Psychology/Religion Pages 144

Optimism *by Helen Keller*   ISBN: *1-59462-108-X*   **$15.95**
Helen Keller was blind, deaf, and mute since 19 months old, yet famously learned how to overcome these handicaps, communicate with the world, and spread her lectures promoting optimism. An inspiring read for everyone...   Biographies/Inspirational Pages 84

Sara Crewe *by Frances Burnett*   ISBN: *1-59462-360-0*   **$9.45**
In the first place, Miss Minchin lived in London. Her home was a large, dull, tall one, in a large, dull square, where all the houses were alike, and all the sparrows were alike, and where all the door-knockers made the same heavy sound...   Childrens/Classic Pages 88

The Autobiography of Benjamin Franklin *by Benjamin Franklin*   ISBN: *1-59462-135-7*   **$24.95**
The Autobiography of Benjamin Franklin has probably been more extensively read than any other American historical work, and no other book of its kind has had such ups and downs of fortune. Franklin lived for many years in England, where he was agent...   Biographies/History Pages 332

Name	
Email	
Telephone	
Address	
City, State ZIP	

☐ Credit Card   ☐ Check / Money Order

Credit Card Number	
Expiration Date	
Signature	

Please Mail to: Book Jungle
                  PO Box 2226
                  Champaign, IL 61825
or Fax to: 630-214-0564

ORDERING INFORMATION

web: *www.bookjungle.com*
email: *sales@bookjungle.com*
fax: *630-214-0564*
mail: *Book Jungle PO Box 2226 Champaign, IL 61825*
or PayPal *to sales@bookjungle.com*

Please contact us for bulk discounts

DIRECT-ORDER TERMS

**20% Discount if You Order
Two or More Books**
Free Domestic Shipping!
Accepted: Master Card, Visa,
Discover, American Express

www.ingramcontent.com/pod-product-compliance
Lightning Source LLC
Chambersburg PA
CBHW081325040426
42453CB00013B/2304